Applying Grace in Marriage

CHARLES R. SWINDOLL

INSIGHT FOR LIVING

APPLYING GRACE IN MARRIAGE

By Charles R. Swindoll

Charles R. Swindoll has devoted his life to the clear, practical teaching and application of God's Word and His grace. Chuck currently is the senior pastor of Stonebriar Community Church in Frisco, Texas, but his listening audience extends far beyond this local church body. As a leading program in Christian broadcasting, *Insight for Living* airs in major Christian radio markets around the world, reaching people groups in languages they can understand. Chuck's extensive writing ministry has also served the body of Christ worldwide and his leadership as president and now chancellor of Dallas Theological Seminary has helped prepare and equip a new generation for ministry.

Copyright © 2006 by Charles R. Swindoll, Inc.

This booklet was written and updated from the original outline and transcript for the message "A Marriage Oiled by Grace" from the series *The Grace Awakening*. Copyright © ℗ 1988 by Charles R. Swindoll, Inc.

"A Marriage Oiled by Grace" was also presented as Chapter Twelve in the book titled *The Grace Awakening* published by Word Publishing, Dallas, Texas. Copyright © 1990, 1996, 2003 by Charles R. Swindoll, Inc.

The original outlines and transcript for "A Marriage Oiled by Grace" were also used as the basis of Chapter Twelve in *The Grace Awakening* study guides published in 1990 and 1996 by Insight for Living, Fullerton, California. This study was updated and revised and published as Chapter Twelve in *The Grace Awakening Workbook* in 2004 by W Publishing Group, A Division of Thomas Nelson, Inc. Copyright 1990, 1996, 2004 by Charles R. Swindoll, Inc.

All rights reserved under international copyright conventions. No portion of this booklet may be reproduced, stored in a retrieval system, or transmitted in any form or by any means—electronic, mechanical, photocopy, recording, or any other—except for brief quotations in printed reviews, without the prior written permission of the publisher.

Published by IFL Publishing House, A Division of Insight for Living
Post Office Box 251007, Plano, Texas 75025-1007

Editor in Chief: Cynthia Swindoll, President, Insight for Living
Executive Vice President: Wayne Stiles, Th.M., D.Min.,
    Dallas Theological Seminary
Editors: Mark Gaither, Th.M., Dallas Theological Seminary
    Jim Craft, B.A., M.A., English, Mississippi College
    Cari Harris, B.A., Journalism, Grand Canyon University
Proofreaders: Melissa Carlisle, M.A., Christian Education,
    Dallas Theological Seminary
    Mike Penn, B.A., Journalism, University of Oklahoma
Cover Designer: Kari Pratt, B.A., Commercial Art,
    Southwestern Oklahoma State University
Production Artist: Nancy Gustine, B.F.A., Advertising Art,
    University of North Texas
Cover Photo: Kari Pratt

Scripture quotations are from the *New American Standard Bible®* (NASB). Copyright © 1960, 1962, 1963, 1968, 1971, 1972, 1973, 1975, 1977, 1995 by The Lockman Foundation. All rights reserved. Used by permission. (www.lockman.org)

An effort has been made to locate sources and obtain permission where necessary for the quotations used in this booklet. In the event of any unintentional omission, a modification will gladly be incorporated in future printings.

ISBN: 978-1-57972-721-5
Printed in the United States of America

Applying Grace in Marriage

A Letter from Chuck

More than fifty years ago, Cynthia and I began a journey together. At the tender ages of twenty and eighteen, we started with great dreams for a great marriage. We were madly in love and couldn't wait to start our lives together. We settled into a nice, small home near the place we both grew up, and I continued my apprenticeship to become a machinist. We faithfully served in our local church, enjoyed good times with our families, and even thought of beginning a little family of our own.

But, as happens to every new couple, life circumstances invaded our little honeymoon existence. I know now why Paul said married people "will have trouble in this life" (1 Corinthians 7:28). We experienced a number of difficulties from outside influences as well as issues we each brought to the union. We soon learned that we couldn't expect youthful exuberance and springtime love to sustain the joy of marriage. Only grace will do that.

Grace is a very difficult concept to comprehend and even harder to apply. The world around us doesn't operate according to grace. "Nothing's for free." "You get what you pay for." "You scratch my back, and I'll scratch yours." "You only get out of something what you put into it." Great advice if you're shopping for a new car or advancing your career. Terrible way to build a marriage.

If both husband and wife can apply grace to their marriage, their home will be a place of security and acceptance, of freedom and fulfillment, of accountability and encouragement. Even if you, alone, will commit to applying grace, you will enjoy a remarkable transformation in your own marriage. As for me, the sweetest place on earth starts about an inch or so inside the door of our home. I absolutely love being there. That has very little to do with the structure or the fixtures or the furniture. My enjoyment has everything to do with the person with whom I share it. The grace we have learned to apply over the years makes our marriage endearing and enduring. The same can be true of yours.

Chuck Swindoll

Charles R. Swindoll

Applying Grace in Marriage

I sometimes wonder what kind of husband Jesus would have made. Of course, He did not sojourn on planet Earth for the purpose of marrying and rearing children, despite the claims of ancient fantasies and modern revisionists. He came to redeem humankind through His death and resurrection. Nevertheless, I imagine that His household would have been much like His Kingdom, a place characterized by grace—a winsome, "yes" kind of place where everyone has the freedom to breathe deeply, slowly, and contentedly.

Strangely, though, the Gospels never once record His using the word *grace*. Of course, He would have used an Aramaic or possibly a Hebrew term, which has the basic meaning, "to bend, to stoop." Grace, then, is a special expression of love. The late pastor and Bible scholar Donald Barnhouse described grace this way: "Love that goes upward is worship; love that goes outward is affection; love that stoops is grace."[1] This is love that expects nothing in return, favor that's offered simply from the goodwill of the giver.

I can think of no better place than marriage where grace should shine brightest, yet it remains conspicuously absent in most marriages today. Grace gives us the ability to encourage our mate, so that by our love, we bring out the best in him or her. Grace is the lubricant that lessens the friction in marriage and keeps the gears of the relationship running smoothly. In this booklet, I hope to so convince you of the essential value of grace in marriage that it will dominate your thoughts in the weeks to come and that it will become an unconscious part of your relationship with your mate. We'll examine Scripture to see how grace affects marital realities, our responsibilities in marriage, and the different yet compatible roles we adopt as husbands and wives.

The Magnetism of Grace

While grace is essential to building a lasting and enjoyable marriage, it has much broader implications. Someone can be a world-class success outside the home, but it is in the secret places of life—intimacy with a spouse being the most private—where he or she is shown to be a person of grace or not. Eugene Peterson, in his fine book titled, *Run with the Horses*, writes,

> Only a few people make the historical headlines, but anyone can

become human. Is it possible to be great when you are taking out the garbage as well as when you are signing a peace treaty? Is it possible to exhibit grace in your conduct in the kitchen as well as in a nationally televised debate?

I once knew a man well who had a commanding public presence and exuded charm to all he met. What he said *mattered*. He had *influence*. He was always impeccably dressed and unfailingly courteous. But his secretary was frequently in tears as a result of his rudely imperious demands. Behind the scenes he was tyrannical and insensitive. His public image was flawless; his personal relationships were shabby.[2]

He lacked grace—grace to be as charming, as courteous, and as careful in his personal relationships, when no one was looking, as when in public. Rest assured, he would eventually be found out. Nevertheless, his lack of grace behind the closed doors of his office revealed the true nature of his character. Anyone he might attract with his public persona would soon be put off by his private lack of grace.

Now, allow me to put this question to you. If your spouse were to tell the honest truth about you, would you be found to be a person of grace? None of us is perfect, but generally speaking, is grace a natural, genuine part of your character? Is your marriage a place of freedom or demands? Blaming or honesty? Peace or defensiveness? Safety or power struggles?

If you'll allow me one more probing question: Does the quality of grace make you attractive to your spouse?

In my preparation for this study, I was encouraged to discover that those people who have left the greatest impact on the lives of others were rarely those who we would consider to be the movers and shakers in society. Stop and think for a moment. Can you name the Secretary of State ten years ago? Can you name the Heisman Trophy winner five years ago? Can you recall who won the Oscar for Best Director four years ago or even the Nobel Peace Prize winner last year? But you will never forget the person who stooped to help you when you were at your lowest. If you are like most, the heroes in your life are not those who flicker across a screen, or set scoring records on the athletic field, or even those who win world acclaim for achievement. Your heroes are those who believed in you when you no longer could, those who loved you without expectation, those who showed you genuine grace.

My plea to you is that you will want to be a hero to your spouse. Someone so characterized by grace that he or she looks forward to being in your presence.

Applying Grace to Marital Realities

In the beginning of the relationship, grace was probably easy to give, and it was abundant in return. And that can reinforce the youthful idealism that most of us have when leaving for the honeymoon. We had found the partner of our dreams, and we fully expected to give and receive everything we have always wanted in marriage. However, in all of those fantasies, the word *duty* never came up. Yet according to 1 Corinthians 7:3–5, a passage that addresses marital intimacy—intimacy in sex, experience, conversation, and affection—we see terms like *duty* and *authority*. Not exactly the words you use on Valentine's Day.

> The husband must fulfill his duty to his wife, and likewise also the wife to her husband. The wife does not

have authority over her own body, but the husband does; and likewise also the husband does not have authority over his own body, but the wife does. Stop depriving one another, except by agreement for a time, so that you may devote yourselves to prayer, and come together again so that Satan will not tempt you because of your lack of self-control. (1 Corinthians 7:3–5)

Paul points to no less than three realities that wise, mature husbands and wives must address as they choose to apply grace in marriage.

Marriage Requires Mutual Unselfishness

Read the passage again, and take note of the words *duty*, *authority*, and *depriving*. The context of Paul's comments extends beyond the issue of physical intimacy, though sex is clearly central. What does it take to operate unselfishly with something as delicate and as personal as sex? It takes grace. Grace to accept. Grace to respect. Grace to be vulnerable. Grace to understand. Grace to affirm. Grace to restrain. Grace to give. And grace to receive with gratitude. Applying grace to marriage requires that we begin with unselfishness.

Marriage is a continual exercise in unselfishness. Because grace gives without expectation, we must be willing to lay aside our own rights and focus our energies on fulfilling those of our partner. That means giving without expecting him or her to fulfill our needs—desires we have a biblical right to claim—in return for doing what is right. Giving in order to get is not grace. It's a bargain in which the other party has not been informed of the terms. To then turn resentful later is doubly unfair.

Grace accepts the reality that the rights of another outweigh our own and that marriage requires unselfishness.

Marriage Requires a Lifelong Commitment

> But to the married I give instructions, not I, but the Lord, that the wife should not leave her husband (but if she does leave, she must remain unmarried, or else be reconciled to her husband), and that the husband should not divorce his wife. But to the rest I say, not the Lord, that if any brother has a wife who is an unbeliever, and she consents to live with him, he must not divorce her. And a

woman who has an unbelieving husband, and he consents to live with her, she must not send her husband away. (1 Corinthians 7:10–13)

This should go without saying, but we have to accept the Word of God at face value and declare: *Marriage is a lifelong commitment.* This will, undoubtedly, require grace to accept — for some more than others. At the wedding ceremony, everyone genuinely adopts the vows he or she utters before God and witnesses. But when circumstances change, dreams are shattered, expectations surrendered, and the reality of living with another sinner sinks in, I'm amazed at how quickly some will begin to rationalize away those promises. Certainly there are a very few valid reasons for divorce, but our duty is first to think of all the reasons to stay committed to the marriage. Too often the reasons to end it come to mind first.

Paul underscores his point in two ways. First by repetition. "The wife should not leave her husband" (7:10); "the husband should not divorce his wife" (7:11); "he must not divorce her" (7:12); "she must not send her husband away" (7:13). One command is sufficient. Two would be eloquent. Three is emphatic, but repeating a command four times is rare in Scripture. (Really, the command appears five times if you count verse 27!) In God's vocabulary, *permanent* means "permanent."

Paul also underscores the point by answering a reasonable objection. Notice the point of verses 12–13. Even a condition in which a believing spouse is bound to an unbeliever provides no reason to end the marriage.

One way that Cynthia and I decided to apply grace in our marriage from the very earliest days was to remove the word *divorce* from our vocabulary. I cannot adequately describe the good that it has done for our bond—to know that, even in the most heated arguments, each of us can count on the other to hammer out our difficulties without ultimatums or one of us packing a suitcase. It isn't easy to stand fast when your feet want to run, but grace is an investment that always pays dividends, sooner or later.

Marriage Includes Troublous Times

> Are you bound to a wife? Do not seek to be released. Are you released from a wife? Do not seek a wife. But if you marry, you have not sinned; and if a virgin marries, she has not sinned. Yet such will have trouble

in this life, and I am trying to spare you. (1 Corinthians 7:27–28)

Paul's last sentence might look somewhat cynical at first glance, but we have to take his context into account. He wrote to a church experiencing a number of difficulties. He described their situation as their "present distress" (7:26). In recommending that single people, whether married previously or not, should remain single, he acknowledges the fact that married people double their distress. As a married couple, any circumstance that afflicts one partner afflicts the other. Remaining single reduces the chances of experiencing difficulty, leaving the single person better able to focus on ministry. Therefore, Paul says, in effect, "Don't shop for a spouse. Don't traffic the singles groups to find another mate. If the Lord wants you married, He will bring one to you. In the meantime, enjoy your freedom to serve Him without the duties and the hardships of marriage."

Additionally, "[married people] will have trouble in this life." Every couple leaving on a honeymoon should have that posted on their dashboard: *Such will have trouble*. Every wife who thinks she has found in her man the answer to all her fears and insecurities needs to know: *Such will have trouble*. Every husband who expects that he has married *the* woman who will always make him feel like a man should be reminded: *Such will have trouble.*

It takes grace to accept that marriage includes troublous times. Since almost no newlywed accepts that truth, it will take grace to get through those times when they arrive. Trouble from calamities. Trouble from disease. Trouble from the old, sinful nature. Trouble from children. Trouble from church squabbles. Trouble from relationships. Trouble from neighbors. Trouble from the times in which we live. Trouble from the weather. Trouble from the car. Trouble from the school.

During some of our most troublous times, Cynthia has taken my hand, looked me square in the eye, and said, "Honey, we'll make it through this." That's grace.

Applying Grace to Marital Responsibilities

Therefore be careful how you walk, not as unwise men but as wise, making the most of your time, because the days are evil. So then do not be foolish, but understand what the will of the Lord is. And do not get drunk with wine, for that is dissipation, but be filled with the Spirit, speaking to one another in psalms and hymns and spiritual songs, singing and making melody with your heart to the Lord; always giving thanks for all things in the name of our Lord Jesus Christ to God, even the Father; and be subject to one another in the fear of Christ. (Ephesians 5:15–21)

This passage begins with Paul's concern for how the Ephesian Christians give expression to their beliefs. He urges them to use wisdom and to let the Lord have complete control of their lives. "Be careful how you walk." Allow the Spirit to guide your steps rather than foolishness. That involves offering encouragement (5:19), giving thanks (5:20), and adopting an attitude of mutual submission (5:21). These are commands that specifically explain how one is to be "filled with the Spirit." These are some of the responsibilities that members of a community have toward one another.

He then applies these principles to married men and women, providing a more detailed description of their responsibilities to each other.

The Responsibility of the Wife

> Wives, be subject to your own husbands, as to the Lord. For the husband is the head of the wife, as Christ also is the head of the church, He Himself being the Savior of the body. But as the church is subject to Christ, so also the wives ought to be to their husbands in everything. (Ephesians 5:22–24)

So much has been said about this passage and its meaning for us today—some of it incorrect, all of it controversial. Unfortunately, space does not permit me to give this the thorough theological treatment it deserves. So let me blend the thoughts of this passage with those of 1 Peter 3 (which we'll study in just a moment) to offer this:

THE WIFE'S PRIMARY RESPONSIBILITY IS TO KNOW HERSELF SO WELL AND RESPECT HERSELF SO MUCH, THAT SHE GIVES HERSELF TO HER HUSBAND WITHOUT HESITATION.

Grace, in this context, creates a sweet, Spirit-filled environment in which no one feels the need to struggle for authority or assert one's rights. Just as the Spirit inspires faith in the church's sovereign protection under the Son, so the wife can willingly release her desire to control, or manipulate, or subvert, or obtain what she desires through her own devices. She can trust that the Lord will meet her needs, which gives her enough security to give herself completely to her husband without reservation or hesitation. Notice that this begins with receiving dignity and self-worth from her relationship with the Lord first, then allowing her husband to provide that support as the Lord develops him.

I am enough of a realist to know that the call for that much grace is a tall order for some women. Believe me; I have met many a husband who make me shudder to think what their wives must have to endure and the grace they must summon in order to honor their husbands as the Lord commands. Christ must be in complete control of your life with the Holy Spirit energizing your actions and your attitudes—your thought processes, your reactions, the words you choose, and even the boundaries you set for yourself. Remember that grace is loving the unlovely with no expectation of anything in return, not even gratitude. And part of what makes grace a spiritual discipline, a quality arising from the Spirit, is that it makes little sense in a world given to sin and selfishness. It will require faith.

The Responsibility of the Husband

> Husbands, love your wives, just as Christ also loved the church and gave Himself up for her, so that He might sanctify her, having cleansed her by the washing of water with the word, that He might present to Himself the church in all her glory, having no spot or wrinkle or any such thing; but that she would be holy and blameless. So husbands ought also to love their own wives as their own bodies. He who loves his own wife loves himself; for no one ever hated his own flesh, but nourishes and cherishes it, just as Christ also does the church, because we are members of His body. For this reason a man shall leave his father and mother and shall be joined to his wife, and the two shall become one flesh. This mystery is great; but I am speaking with reference to Christ and the church. (Ephesians 5:25–32)

I am sometimes hesitant to address wives about submission in the hearing of husbands because we can become a little smug about it. Some take the point of verses 22–24 as the Lord's authorization to assume a domineering position. In counseling many couples over the years, I have found that when a husband pays *any* attention to the issue of submission, I am seeing a power play in action. A husband who has this passage in clear perspective tends to skip right past verses 22–24, eager to absorb and apply verses 25–32.

In Paul's day, the "submission" portion of the passage did little to change the responsibility of wives in the marriage relationship. The verses that followed, however, radically altered the responsibility of the husband. The Greek and Roman concept of a patriarch viewed the household as a miniature kingdom with the husband as king. In Christ's kingdom, the King assumed a servant's role as least of all, placing the needs of the entire kingdom above His own—even to the extreme of sacrificing His own life. "Husbands," the Lord says in effect, "if you want to be king, follow My example."

Blending the thoughts of Ephesians 5:25–32 and 1 Peter 3 as I did before, I arrive at the following:

> **THE HUSBAND'S PRIMARY RESPONSIBILITY IS TO LOVE THE LORD AND LIKE HIMSELF SO COMPLETELY THAT HE CAN GIVE HIMSELF TO HIS WIFE WITHOUT CONDITIONS.**

This, again, is an act of grace—love without conditions. Husbands must remove the word *if* from their vocabulary. "If you will do . . . If you will say . . . If you will respond, then I will give myself." Altering the quality of our love based on the actions of others is not leadership. In choosing to abdicate our leadership role in this way, we may fail to love our wives as the Lord commands or even as much as we desire. I have stood alongside men who have buried their wives sooner than they had expected, and almost without exception, I've had them fall on my shoulder in tears and say, "Why? Why did it take this to reveal to me what I had in my wife? Why did I not show her the love I felt while she was alive?"

Men like these probably place conditions on their love, waiting for the right motives, holding back until an unspoken set of expectations is fulfilled before giving themselves. Rather than loving their wives "as their own bodies," their love becomes a tool in a game to establish control and maintain dominance. And the long-term harm can be devastating to women.

Kevin Leman has written a very insightful book titled, *The Pleasers: Women Who Can't Say No—and the Men Who Control Them*. I find his observations to be a stinging indictment of many—if not most—husbands.

The cost of marriage is higher for wives than for husbands. If you are talking about good mental health and psychological well-being, the men have it better every time.

Despite all of their complaints about marriage, more women than men find marriage a source of happiness. They cling to marriage regardless of the cost.

Down through the centuries women have been the pleasers, men the controllers. Robert Karen, who conducts workshops for men and women on power and intimacy, refers to the "old" and "new" systems of male/female relationships. Our parents and grandparents knew a world that had stabler values and much more clearly defined roles for men and women. Power and responsibility were clearly assigned, and everyone knew where he or she stood. The system was often unfair to women but it did offer them a certain amount of security. If a woman was willing to accept the ground rules and the limits that marriage imposed on her, she could be quite happy.

A woman's job was to keep the home, raise the children, and be there for the whole family. The man's job was to go out and earn the living and "make contributions to society." Men were, in effect, put on a pedestal and wives were relegated to second-class citizenship.

Enter women's liberation in the latter part of the twentieth century, and all this inequality is supposed to be dying out—but is it?

Women are finding that "having it all" is nothing that special. In fact, they're catching up with the men in having heart disease, ulcers, and other stress-related illnesses. Now they are allowed to get good jobs and earn excellent incomes, but the emotional balance of power at home is still much the same.

Most women still do the giving, while the men continue to take. The woman is the one who is more

> capable of compassion, support, and being there when needed. Men still aren't in touch with their feelings the way women are. They are less capable of reaching out to make emotional contact. But they are very capable of reaching out to take whatever a woman has to offer, and in so doing, they often take advantage.[3]

Dr. Leman refers to a "pleaser" as the moth and a "controller" as the flame. In some ways, this arrangement is built into the basic constitution of women and men, yet sin has twisted this potentially beautiful interaction into something grotesque. The Lord never intended women to please at any cost, neither did He expect men to consume that desire like a fire.

The respective responsibilities of the husband and wife must be infused and animated by grace. I find that the more I understand and apply grace, the less I desire to possess authority and the less I am threatened by the authority of others. As I imitate Christ's love for the church, affirming and releasing my wife from my controlling grip, Cynthia's respect for me grows beyond what I could ever gain by demanding it.

If this free exchange of grace takes place, Paul's command in Ephesians 5:33 hardly becomes necessary: "Nevertheless, each individual among you also is to love his own wife even as himself, and the wife must see to it that she respects her husband." Grace grants freedom to others. Grace enhances the dignity of another. Grace forgives the failure of another to respond as he or she should. Grace, when applied to marriage, gives each partner greater opportunity to fulfill his or her basic responsibility.

Applying Grace to Marital Roles

We live during a time when the basic roles of husband and wife have become blurred. Men are afraid to be men, and women are ashamed to be women. Peter's letter to Christians scattered throughout the Roman Empire contains guidelines that help to reestablish those distinct roles according to God's original design. In 1 Peter 3:1–7, we see genuine femininity described as certain character traits that are precious to the Lord and impressive for a husband. We also see a masculinity that strengthens the home and gives dignity to a wife. Again, this is grace on display in the home.

In the same way, you wives, be submissive to your own husbands so that even if any of them are disobedient to the word, they may be won without a word by the behavior of their wives, as they observe your chaste and respectful behavior. Your adornment must not be merely external—braiding the hair, and wearing gold jewelry, or putting on dresses; but let it be the hidden person of the heart, with the imperishable quality of a gentle and quiet spirit, which is precious in the sight of God. For in this way in former times the holy women also, who hoped in God, used to adorn themselves, being submissive to their own husbands; just as Sarah obeyed Abraham, calling him lord, and you have become her children if you do what is right without being frightened by any fear. You husbands in the same way, live with your wives in an understanding way, as with someone weaker, since she is a woman; and show her honor as a fellow heir of the grace of life, so that your prayers will not be hindered. (1 Peter 3:1–7)

The Role of the Wife

In a context of submission (and once again, this beautiful relationship that has been cultivated with the Lord Jesus now finds expression in the home), we see a wife who finds delight in giving herself so completely to obeying the Lord even if her husband doesn't. Take note of the result: A husband who is inspired to obey Christ, having observed his wife's wholehearted devotion to doing what is right and having observed her respect for himself. The word *observe* in this verse means "to carefully watch." Think of a referee reviewing a disputed call on instant replay. He slows the film down to see the action frame by frame so that he can be sure of what he sees in order to make the right judgment about it. But don't mistake what he's watching. The tendency of a great many women is to substitute external seductiveness for internal beauty.

Now, I've heard preachers go crazy with verse 3, "braiding the hair, and wearing gold jewelry, or putting on dresses," suggesting that those are sinful. "Don't braid your hair." "Don't wear gold jewelry." I never hear them finish with, "Don't wear dresses!" Obviously, this is not the correct interpretation. The emphasis should be placed on the word *merely*. A husband feels very honored — even loved — when his wife puts effort into looking beautiful for him. He enjoys the results, but far more than that, he feels honored by the effort. The Lord doesn't mean for a woman to walk around looking like an unmade bed as evidence of a pure heart. The warning here is to avoid substituting adornment for character.

> **THE WIFE'S ROLE IS TO MODEL TRUE FEMININITY WITH CHARACTER TRAITS THAT ARE PRECIOUS TO GOD AND IMPRESSIVE TO HER HUSBAND.**

The evidence of genuine femininity is an incorruptible, gentle, and tranquil spirit. When a husband experiences this in his wife, it inspires him to be genuinely masculine.

The Role of the Husband

The words *in the same way* at the top of Peter's instructions to women point back to a general command for all Christians in 1 Peter 2:17. "Honor all people, love the brotherhood, fear God, honor the king." "In the same way" begins Peter's instruction for men.

"Live with" comes from a single, Greek term that places great emphasis on the "with" part of that command. This means more than eating and staring at a television in a shared living space. The literal command in Greek is "with-live your wife according to knowledge." This means that a husband must really know his wife. He knows her like no one else knows her. He knows her deepest hurts, her most troublesome fears, and the things that give her the greatest joy. He knows precisely how to affirm and encourage her so that she feels cherished.

The description "someone weaker" is literally, "weaker vessel" in the original language. But this should not be read to imply inferiority. The idea is "more fragile." In our home, we have everyday dishes that we can throw into the microwave, toss into the dishwasher, and stack in the cabinets. They're tough enough to withstand casual abuse, and if they break, we can easily replace them. Now, if I want to be in a whole heap of trouble, all I have to do is give Cynthia's fine china the same treatment! Why? Because they are fragile and precious. In fact, we have a whole piece of furniture dedicated to display their delicate beauty and keep them safe.

That should be the picture of a husband. He is to be her safe place. A woman has to be tough at work. She has to be resilient and tireless with the children. She must be strong in her daily interactions with other people. As a result, she craves a safe place to find shelter—a place to vent her emotions without hearing a logical response, a place to be "unreasonable" without chiding or lecturing, a place to be understood without advice, a place to cry without someone feeling responsible for the sadness and frustration.

Frank Minirth put it this way:

> In my experience, the best marriages tend to be those where the husband is able to put aside his urge to offer answers or plans of action and simply listen with compassion. More often than not, advice only puts him on the side of the problem in his wife's eyes, which men find bewildering.
>
> Wise men know the power of listening. A woman's greatest desire is to be heard and understood by her man. What happens after that is almost inconsequential. One woman said, "Most of the time I don't want him to say or do anything. I just want him to be fighting mad along with me. Then I can solve my own problems." [4]

Provide that kind of an environment for your wife, husbands, and you will captivate her heart.

This is the freedom that grace creates, a kind of grace that a husband can provide as he faithfully fulfills his role.

> **THE HUSBAND'S ROLE IS TO PROVIDE GENUINE MASCULINITY, UNSELFISH AND SENSITIVE LEADERSHIP THAT STRENGTHENS THE HOME AND GIVES DIGNITY TO HIS WIFE.**

A Word of Warning

Grace, if it is genuine, always includes the danger of abuse. How tempting it is for a wife to so delight in the provision and protection of a good man that she becomes like a little girl looking for a daddy in her husband. I have seen some wives become helpless and irresponsible, expecting their husband to assume more and more responsibility. I have seen them avoid carrying their share of the family load, choosing to avoid the risk of failure, and calling it submission. And they are usually masters at manipulation.

I have seen men abuse grace as well. Some husbands are fortunate enough to find a strong, supportive partner who willingly takes on responsibility and contributes one hundred percent of what she has, and he rewards her grace with laziness. Some men become little boys hoping his wife will assume the role of mother, clean up his messes, meet his shifting emotions with pampering, make all his decisions, and ask no questions about his financial irresponsibility. Furthermore, they become petty and critical, and take the gift of a helpmeet for granted.

Grace is always risky. Grace always gives ample room for abuse. Grace very often comes at great expense to the giver. Grace always involves the exercise of faith. Nevertheless, grace is the only way to enjoy marriage as God intended. When both partners apply grace to their marriage, each lacks nothing and feels little need to focus on self. The husband gives his life to his mate and she, in turn, gives it back.

Practical Grace in Marriage

Dr. Willard Harley wrote a fine book many years ago titled, *His Needs, Her Needs*. Having studied data from twenty years of counseling experience and more than fifteen thousand questionnaires, he saw a distinct pattern that led him to produce two lists: the five primary relationship needs of women and the five primary relationship needs of men. Naturally, this represents the majority of women and men, which means that a significant number of couples will have different needs. But these offer good direction if you want to give practical application to grace in your marriage.

For Women

Affection: tender, non-sexual expressions that convey the message: *I'll take care of you and protect you, you are important to me, I am concerned about the problems you face, and I think you're wonderful.* This can be a warm hug, a thoughtful note, holding hands, or a bouquet of flowers.[5] Touching can be intimate, but it must communicate that the husband values the wife as precious to him for reasons other than sexual fulfillment.

Conversation: talk that leads to her knowing the inner life of her husband and her feeling understood by him. Conversation is to a woman what physical intimacy is to a man. And just like love-making, the process is more important to creating a bond than the result.

> "George, let's talk."
>
> "What would you like to talk about?"
>
> George's innocent inquiry would raise the ire of most women. . . . He

might understand [her] aggravation better if she had a conversation like this with him:

"Mary, let's make love."

"Why, George? Are we ready to have children?" [6]

The process of communication—not merely its result—is how a wife feels loved, cared for, appreciated, respected, and wanted. When a husband suddenly shuts off communication, the emotional effect can be devastating to her. She feels cast aside and wonders if he still loves her.

Honesty and openness: communication that accurately reflects the husband's feelings and motives. A wife must be able to trust her husband completely. Failure to be genuine about his past, present, and future destroys her sense of security. "When a husband honestly communicates with his wife, it allows her to contemplate the future more accurately and to plan accordingly—two very important factors for most women." [7]

Financial support: sufficient financial provision from the husband (not including any income she earns) to maintain a lifestyle similar to that of the wife's original home. This allows her to feel supported and cared for, safe from the perils of sudden poverty.

Family commitment: meaningful involvement in the care of what the wife prizes most. "Wives want their husbands to take a leadership role in [the] family and to commit themselves to the moral and educational development of the children."[8]

For Men

Sexual fulfillment: physical intimacy in which the wife is actively engaged and satisfied. Quantity is important but not nearly as much as the emotions involved. "In a very deep way, your man often feels isolated and burdened by secret feelings of inadequacy. Making love with you assures him that you find him desirable, salves a deep sense of loneliness, and gives him the strength and well-being necessary to face the world with confidence. . . . The survey showed that even if they were getting all the sex they wanted, three out of four men would still feel empty if their wife wasn't both engaged and satisfied. . . . At the most basic level, your man wants to be wanted."[9]

Recreational companionship: a playmate with whom to enjoy life. Men tend to establish bonds with other people through shared activity. "[Wives] may encourage their husbands to continue their recreational activities without them. I consider that option very dangerous to a marriage, because men place surprising importance on having their wives as recreational companions."[10] To take an active interest in a husband's activities is to take an interest in *him*. "Playing with their wives makes [men] feel close and loving and intimate; it offers an escape from the ordinary, a time to focus on each other—all things that women also want from romance."[11]

An attractive spouse: the desire and demonstrated effort to look good for the husband. The husband was not attracted to and didn't fall in love with a swimsuit model. He is attracted to his wife, so "an attractive spouse" is one who takes care of herself. "Since men are so visual, seeing [their wives] make the effort to look good makes them feel loved and cared for."[12]

Domestic support: help in maintaining a tranquil, orderly household. While most husbands expect to share household duties, he needs to be free of being overwhelmed by them. Home, to a man, represents a place of comfort and peace, a shelter from the chaos he must face each day.

Admiration: respect for the husband's judgment, abilities, and character, along with verbal expressions of respect for him, both public and private. To say, "I respect you" to a man is very much the same as saying, "I love you." In a recent survey, three out of four men given a choice between feeling disrespected and unloved would rather feel unloved.[13]

―

First Peter 3:7 includes the phrase, "show her honor as a fellow heir of the grace of life." The literal Greek for "fellow heir" is co-receiver. This points to equality and mutuality. Mutual and equal dignity. Mutual and equal humility. Mutual and equal grace. You and your spouse have at your disposal all the grace you could ever want. But as God has designed it, you must offer it to one another. Neither partner can demand grace or expect grace in return. Each must offer it freely.

Mutual grace applied to marriage can make a home—and a relationship—serve as a little taste of heaven. In other words, if both husband and wife can apply grace to their marriage, their home will be a place of safety and security, joy and contentment, freedom and fulfillment, encouragement and love. Be encouraged—the effort required to apply grace is far outweighed by its reward.

May the grace of our Lord Jesus Christ, the love of God and the fellowship and peace of His Holy Spirit rest and abide upon our hearts and, yes, upon our homes, now and forevermore. Amen.

We Are Here for You

If you desire to find out more about knowing God and His plan for you in the Bible, contact us. Insight for Living provides staff pastors and women's counselors who are available for free written correspondence or phone consultation. These seminary-trained and seasoned men and women have years of pastoral experience and are well-qualified guides for your spiritual journey.

Please feel welcome to contact our Pastoral Ministries department by calling the Insight for Living Care Line: 972-473-5097, 8 A.M. through 5 P.M. Central Time. Or you may write to the following address:

> Insight for Living
> Pastoral Ministries Department
> Post Office Box 269000
> Plano, Texas 75026-9000

Endnotes

1. Donald Grey Barnhouse, *Man's Ruin: Exposition of Bible Doctrines, Taking the Epistle to the Romans as a Point of Departure*, vol. 1, *Romans 1:1–32* (Grand Rapids: Wm. B. Eerdmans, 1952), 72.

2. Eugene H. Peterson, *Run with the Horses: The Quest for Life at Its Best* (Downers Grove, Ill.: InterVarsity, 1983), 159–160.

3. Keven Leman, *The Pleasers: Women Who Can't Say No—and the Men Who Control Them* (Old Tappan, NJ: Fleming H. Revell, 1987), 287–288.

4. Frank & Mary Alice Minirth, *Secrets of a Strong Marriage: 99 Time-Tested Truths to Make Your Love Last a Lifetime* (Colorado Springs: Cook Communications Ministries, 2005), 43–44.

5. Willard F. Harley, Jr., *His Needs, Her Needs: Building an Affair-proof Marriage* (Old Tappan, NJ: Fleming H. Revell, 1986), 29–30.

6. Harley, 61.

7. Harley, 90.

8. Harley, 140.

9. Shaunti Feldhahn, *For Women Only: What You Need to Know about the Inner Lives of Men* (Sisters, Ore.: Multnomah, 2004), 92–94.

10. Harley, 74.

11. Feldhahn, 146–147.

12. Feldhahn, 165.

13. Feldhahn, 22–23.